Seashells & Beachcombing for Kids

An Introduction to Beach Life of the Atlantic, Gulf, and Pacific Coasts

Stephanie Panlasigui and Erika Zambello

PUBLICATIONS
Adventure
an imprint of Adventure**KEEN**

Disclaimer Kids should always be accompanied by an adult when outdoors, especially near the ocean. Life jackets are essential when swimming, and always be aware of potentially hazardous conditions, such as riptides, heavy surf, treacherous currents, sneaker waves, and potentially dangerous marine animals. It's your responsibility to recognize, and avoid, the potentially dangerous bugs, insects, plants, or animals in your area. Always be aware of the weather and your surroundings, and stay off private property.

Edited by Brett Ortler

Cover and book design by Jonathan Norberg

Proofread by Ritchey Halphen and Andrew Mollenkof

Photo credits
Front cover: **Daniel Novak/Shutterstock:** conch; **Good luck images/Shutterstock:** starfish; **icemanphotos/Shutterstock:** beach waves; **John Wijsman/Shutterstock:** corner gull; **Jonathan Norberg:** Hand; **thawatchai lappuchudom/Shutterstock:** shells in hand; **wattana/Shutterstock:** sand ripples.

Back cover and spine: **Elliot Rusty Harold/Shutterstock:** Sea Nettle; **fotosteve/Shutterstock:** Brown Pelican; **Good luck images/Shutterstock:** shell

credits continued on page 143

10 9 8 7 6 5 4 3 2 1
Seashells & Beachcombing for Kids
Copyright © 2023 by Stephanie Panlasigui and Erika Zambello
Published by Adventure Publications, an imprint of AdventureKEEN
310 Garfield Street South
Cambridge, Minnesota 55008
(800) 678-7006
www.adventurepublications.net
All rights reserved
Printed in China
Cataloging-in-Publication data is available from the Library of Congress
ISBN 978-1-64755-323-4 (pbk.); ISBN 978-1-64755-324-1 (ebook)

Thank you to our families and friends who have gone on countless adventures with us and supported us year after year.

—Stephanie Panlasigui and Erika Zambello

We would like to acknowledge that the places we explore on the Atlantic and Pacific Coasts, and throughout North America, are the ancestral lands of Indigenous peoples. Many places that are now designated as parks, wildlife refuges, and other conservation lands were founded upon exclusions and erasures of many sovereign nations. We encourage you to learn more about the Indigenous peoples on whose lands you live, learn, play, and explore. A helpful place to start is the website Native Land (https://native-land.ca) to learn the names of these sovereign nations. But don't stop there—learn more about the ways each nation continues to live in connection with nature to this day and into the future.

Table of Contents

A Word From the Authors

Beaches may be narrow, but they are full of drama. From crashing waves to iconic wildlife, beaches are a window into not only our oceans but our own human behavior as well.

We are drawn to the beaches by birds. Gulls, terns, tiny sandpipers that run along the surf. Birds of all shapes and sizes have become skilled at using the beaches to not only find food but also find mates and raise their chicks.

Once you start looking at birds, you realize how much more there is to see! The birds feed on fish swimming just a few inches from shore, or on tiny crustaceans, clams, or worms just below the sand. That seaweed you see washing up from the waves? It's full of food

not just for birds but for so many creatures! The more you really explore and study the beaches, the more discoveries you can make. We love that each time we hit the sand, there is an opportunity to learn something new.

Beaches may not seem vulnerable, but they are, and it's up to us to protect them. We need to make sure we keep trash off the sand, and we need to work across cities, states, and countries to reduce the sea level rise that could flood these marvelous places. Already so many homes and businesses have been built on beach dunes—we must protect what is left for the plants and animals that need these places to survive.

We hope you love the beaches as much as we do!

Beach Basics

WHAT IS A BEACH?

A beach is the place where land meets a body of water, and sand builds up over time. When you think of a beach, you might think of a long, narrow strip of sand along the ocean, but beaches can also form along lakes or even rivers. But ocean beaches are the most widespread and probably the most well known.

PARTS OF A BEACH

Supratidal Zone

This area may be splashed by waves during high tide, but it is almost never completely under water.

Drift Line or Wrack Line

This area or "line" is where shells or seagrass are left on the beach during high tide.

Intertidal Zone

This section of the beach is underwater during high tide, but it is exposed during low tide. It is often

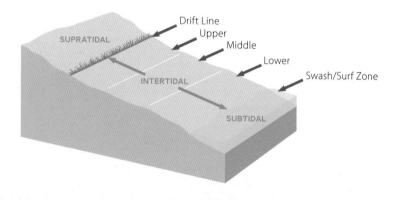

divided into three zones: Upper, Middle, and Lower. Because conditions change frequently in the Intertidal Zone, it can be a difficult place to live, yet many species have adapted to living here.

Swash/Surf Zone
This zone is where waves crash into the sand.

Subtidal Zone
This zone is always covered by salt water.

Barrier Island
Barrier islands run parallel (sideways) to the coastline and are made of shifting sands deposited by currents. They can change shape after storms or over time. They are very important for animals (some of which are specially adapted to living there) and people, as barrier islands often absorb wind and waves from storms and hurricanes.

Sand
Sand is formed from ground-up rock, shell, and fossils, giving different beaches a unique look and feel. Some beaches are famous for pure white sand, while others have pink, black, or even orange sand!

Dune
When sand is held in place by the roots of plants and further sculpted by strong winds, they form hills of sand called *dunes*. Dunes create important habitat for a range of native species, but they are more fragile than they look. Don't walk on them!

HABITATS ON A BEACH

Beaches are home to a wide variety of habitats, or places where animals and plants can live. Here are some of the most well-known types on beaches.

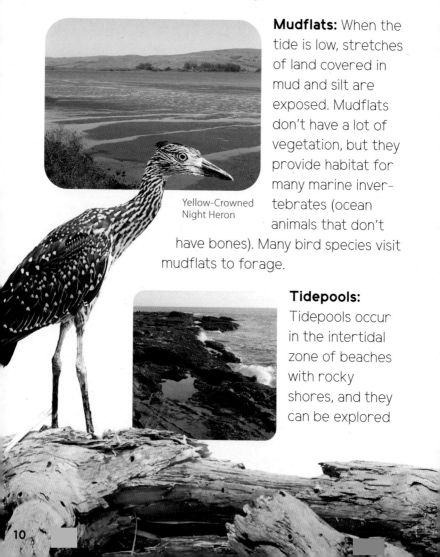

Mudflats: When the tide is low, stretches of land covered in mud and silt are exposed. Mudflats don't have a lot of vegetation, but they provide habitat for many marine invertebrates (ocean animals that don't have bones). Many bird species visit mudflats to forage.

Yellow-Crowned Night Heron

Tidepools: Tidepools occur in the intertidal zone of beaches with rocky shores, and they can be explored

during low tide. Species that live here have adapted to survive difficult conditions, including the force of waves, temperature changes, and long exposure to air and sun. Many tidepools can be found along the Pacific Coast because a lot of the coast has rocky shores. Rocky shores are less common on the Atlantic Coast, but Maine has rocky shores and offers some notable tidepools to explore. (For more on tidepools, see page 114.)

(For more on tidepools, see page 114.)

Mangroves: In Florida, mangrove forests grow right into the water. Mangroves are trees that are specially adapted to wet and salty conditions. Mangroves have prop roots that grow down from the branches for stability. Mangroves provide important habitat to a range of species, including nesting wading birds like herons and egrets, as well as barnacles, fish, and even deer! In fact, 75% species of fish that anglers like to catch in South Florida depend on mangroves for their survival. Did you know that mangroves protect people too? They protect the shoreline—and coastal communities—from erosion during storms and storm surges.

Estuaries: An *estuary* is where a river meets an ocean and the freshwater and saltwater mix. Many unique habitats are found in estuaries. Examples include mangroves (page 11) and salt marshes (below).

Salt Marshes: Salt marshes are low, flat areas that are affected by tides. Grasses and other plants live in salt marshes. This habitat is important for a huge number of birds, and essential as places to rest and feed for the birds that migrate north and south along both coasts on migratory routes called the Atlantic and Pacific Flyways. Salt marshes also offer a safe place for young fish to begin their life. There are many other animals that benefit from salt marshes, including otters, dolphins, and crabs.

UNDERWATER HABITATS

Some habitats are under water and not visible from shore, but signs of life from these ecosystems can wash up on the beach.

Kelp Forest: On the Pacific Coast, kelp forests provide food and shelter to many species, including iconic animals like sea otters and sea lions. Even though kelp looks like a tree and we call these areas forests, kelp is a type of brown algae, not a plant. The kelp's *holdfast* looks like roots and anchors the kelp to the ocean floor. *Floats* are gas-filled bulbs that help the kelp stand upright. Kelp grows extremely fast, up to 1½ feet per day, and kelp can reach 175 feet in length.

Seagrass Meadows: Seagrasses are underwater plants that live in estuaries and oceans. Seagrass meadows are important habitats for fish, sea turtles, manatees, and birds.

Coral Reefs: Coral may look like a rock or a plant, but corals are actually small animals. There are soft corals and hard corals. Hard corals create a hard exoskeleton (exterior skeleton) and are considered

Florida coral reef

to be *reef-building* corals. Coral reefs form over thousands of years, and these massive and important structures have the most biodiversity (different kinds of life-forms) of any marine ecosystem.

Oyster Reefs: Oysters are shellfish that grow on the rocky ocean bottom or on other oyster shells. As they grow on top of each other, the shells accumulate, creating an oyster reef over time where many other invertebrates and fish can shelter and feed.

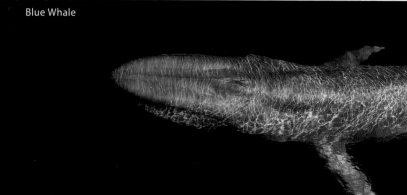
Blue Whale

Whale Shark

Open Ocean: Any area of the ocean beyond the coastal areas is considered open ocean. Some of the biggest animal species live in the open ocean, including great white sharks, humpback whales, and sperm whales. The world's largest animal is the blue whale (below), which can grow to almost 100 feet long and can weigh 400,000 lbs. The world's largest fish is the whale shark (above), which can grow to almost 40 feet long and can live to 150 years old. Both blue whales and whale sharks grow to immense sizes by eating vast amounts of the ocean's tiniest creatures, called *plankton*.

TIDES

Unlike most other bodies of water, oceans are affected by tides. Earth's oceans are huge, and over the course of a day, they are affected by the gravity of the moon and the sun. Tides are essentially long, large waves driven by the gravitational pull of the moon and the sun. When one of these waves reaches its highest point, it's called *high tide*. Later, when the waves recede to their lowest point, it's called *low tide*. Most beaches have two high tides and two low tides per day.

Tides also can bring creatures with them—like sea turtles. These turtles use currents and tides to navigate around the ocean, eventually returning to the beaches where they were born to lay their own eggs.

Have you heard of messages in a bottle? For hundreds of years, people have carefully written messages on slips of paper, sealed them in bottles, and thrown them into the sea, hoping someone would find them someday. These bottles can float in the ocean for a *long* time, but eventually tides carry them to shore once more. In fact, in 2018, Australian beach-goers discovered a message written 132 years

ago! The bottle and message had been thrown over the side of a ship as part of a German experiment to study ocean currents.

Unfortunately, tides can also bring trash to our beaches—or pull trash we have left behind out to sea. Recently, a trash can fell into the ocean in Myrtle Beach, South Carolina, dragged farther into the water by an outgoing tide. In 2021, the trash can reappeared—4,000 miles away in Ireland! The tide had connected the trash can with the Gulf Stream, which in turn carried it all the way to the shores of Ireland.

Still, trash is a huge problem in the ocean, already numbering an estimated 5.25 trillion pieces; 269,000 tons float on the surface, and so much more is now trapped beneath the waves. Because plastic takes hundreds of years to degrade, much of this trash will remain in our oceans for a long time to come. Because of this, we need to make sure no more trash reaches the sea. If you bring items to the beach, take them home. Bring a bag with you to collect any additional trash that you might see during your beach trip, and dispose of it properly. For eating and drinking, choose utensils that can be reused, like metal forks and canteens. Scientists think there could be millions of water bottles in the oceans right now, posing choking hazards to wildlife. Because many sea creatures can't tell the difference between plastic and food, they may eat too much, causing them to get sick or even die.

Date	Day of the Week	Time	Predicted Tide (In Feet)	High/Low
8/14/22	Sunday	3:13 am	0.55	Low
8/14/22	Sunday	7:41 am	2.71	High
8/14/22	Sunday	3:58 pm	−0.17	Low
8/14/22	Sunday	8:50 pm	2.57	High
8/15/22	Monday	4:07 pm	0.61	Low
8/15/22	Monday	8:28 pm	2.44	High
8/15/22	Monday	4:27 pm	−0.04	Low
8/15/22	Monday	9:29 pm	2.69	High

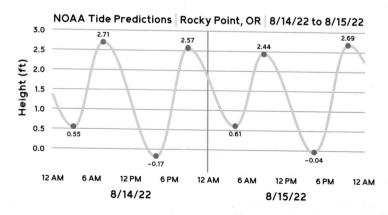

NOAA Tide Predictions | Rocky Point, OR | 8/14/22 to 8/15/22

Because tides can have a major impact on how much of the beach is exposed during your visit, it is always a good idea to check the tide chart before any outing. Tides are predictable, which means scientists can use math to determine when high tide and low tide will occur. Tables that list tide data are available online (tidesandcurrents.noaa.gov/tide_predictions.html). Once you find a tide table online or at a local shop in your area, look up the date you plan to head to the beach and the high- and low-tide times.

Some tide terms to know:

High Tide: When the tide reaches the highest point on the beach for that day, before retreating once more.

Low Tide: When the tide reaches the lowest point on the beach for that day, before surging once more.

Crest: The highest part of a wave.

Neap Tide: These tides are moderate because both the sun and the moon are at right angles to each other; this makes high and low tides closer together than normal.

King Tide: Full moons can bring higher-than-normal tides, called *king tides*. In some areas, king tides can cause flooding.

Note: *Tsunamis* (see pg. 29) are sometimes called tidal waves, but they're completely unrelated to tides. They're actually caused by earthquakes and the like.

CURRENTS

Currents move water from one part of the ocean to another. They always flow in the same direction at a predictable speed, and they move based on a combination of factors, including water, wind, waves, ocean temperature, and more. People have studied currents since the early days of sailing to help them navigate across the oceans.

Along the Atlantic Coast, the Gulf Stream moves warm water from the Gulf of Mexico northward, eventually all the way to Iceland and the United Kingdom. Another current called the Labrador Current narrowly hugs the Atlantic Coast traveling southward. Near the Outer Banks of North Carolina, the Labrador Current and the Gulf Stream meet, and the mixture of warm and cold water moving in opposite directions can create fog and rough waters. These conditions caused over 5,000 shipwrecks in the area now known as the Graveyard of the Atlantic.

Elsewhere in the oceans, currents drive nutrients from one place to another, as well as temperature changes that have become essential for iconic creatures that have adapted to specific ocean conditions. Wildlife depend on currents to bring the nutrient-rich water—and the food it contains—up from the bottom and then around the globe.

For example, along the Pacific Coast, winds blowing along the shore from north to south push water away, and deeper water comes up to take its place. This process, called *upwelling*, occurs in spring and peaks in summer. The deeper water that comes toward the surface tends to be colder and richer with nutrients. These nutrients support the growth of seaweed and plankton that are eaten by many fish, birds, and other animals.

It's not just ocean creatures that depend on ocean currents—we do too. Ocean currents take warm water from the tropics and move it both north and south toward the earth's poles. As a result, the entire planet has a more moderate climate. Without the currents, temperatures would be much more extreme (either hot or cold).

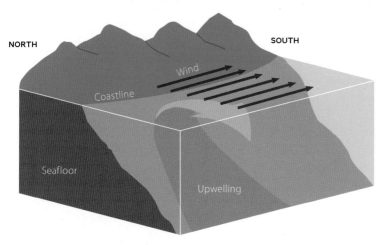

During upwelling, wind-displaced surface waters are replaced by cold, nutrient-rich water that rises up from below.
Figure modified by D. Reed from image by J. Wallace and S. Vogel, *El Niño and Climate Prediction*. Image courtesy of Sanctuary Quest 2002, NOAA/OER.

Climate change has already altered many of these critical ocean currents, speeding them up. These faster currents won't be able to absorb as much heat, which instead will remain in the atmosphere. Moreover, the wildlife species that live in these surface environments—where much of the heating and speeding will occur—will have to adapt to changing conditions or go extinct.

Climate change affects more than the Gulf Stream—it also makes hurricanes (such as Hurricane Katrina, shown below in an NOAA satellite photo) become more frequent and intense.

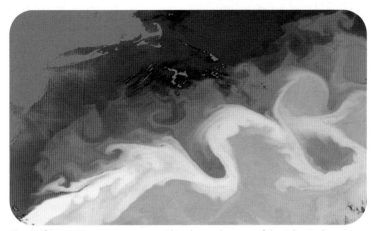

The Gulf Stream is a warm current within the cool waters of the Atlantic Ocean. This NASA satellite photo of the Gulf Stream shows the water temperature: purple for colder water and yellow for warmer water.

There is an exception to this: the Gulf Stream. The Gulf Stream current might actually be slowing down as ice from the Arctic continues to melt. The addition of ice water to the surrounding ocean in turn makes the water less salty and less likely to sink to the bottom of the ocean. This interferes with how the Gulf Stream works.

SAND COLOR AND WATER COLOR

Different regions have beaches with different types of sand. Sand is created in different ways, and it is made up of tiny fragments of rock, fossil or shell.

Brown/Yellow Sand: Sand of these colors are made up of a mix of different minerals. When rivers are the source of the gravel for the sand, the sand is finer (smaller). When glaciers are the source, there are larger grains and more pebbles.

Black Sand: Sand of these colors are made up of a mix of different minerals. The black sand on some beaches comes from igneous rocks (volcanic rocks).

Quartz Sand: Often called "sugar sand" because it looks like sugar, this type originates from quartz, which gives it a bright white color.

Coquina (Orange): Some sand is even orange. Daytona Beach is a famous example, and the color comes from ground-up rock known as *coquina.* Coquina is made up of the shells of many different kinds of sea creatures. When the coquina breaks down, it turns to sand. It gets its rusty color from the presence of iron (a mineral).

Feldspar: An abundant mineral, feldspar makes up much of the sand on beaches as you head farther north up the Atlantic Ocean coastline.

Why does water look different at the beach? Sand! When you hold a glass of water in your hand, the water looks clear. At the beach, you can see the water appear bluer and darker. The color of sand and rocks can also affect the water color you see. For example, white rocks and sand make the water look bright turquoise blue at some beaches. Floating sand and debris stirred up by wave action, or an abundance of microscopic organisms in the water called *zooplankton* and *phytoplankton,* can also give water a murky look.

The bright-white sand and shallow waters of this Florida beach give the water its brilliant turquoise color.

The water gets deeper closer to shore in this part of the Maine coast. The depth of the water and the brown rocks make the water appear dark blue.

BEACH SAFETY

Beaches are fun, exciting places, but at the beach, visitors are exposed to sun, wind, and water, so it's good to prepare for your visit. Here are a few things to consider.

Surf, Tides, and Other Conditions

Before you head to the beach, check the conditions of the place you want to visit. You want to know how high or low the tide will be during the visit, the surf (wave) conditions, and weather conditions. The surf report will tell you how big the waves are. The weather forecast will help you gather the right clothes and supplies for the day.

If lightning is in your weather forecast, it may be unsafe to visit the beach. If you are already at the beach and you hear thunder or see lightning, get out of the water immediately and find a place to take shelter away from the water.

Your local weather forecast may include a UV index, which tells you strong UV (ultraviolet) rays are in your area. UV rays come from the sun, and even on a cloudy day UV rays can cause a sunburn and other damage to your skin.

Lifeguards

Lifeguards are trained to make sure everyone at the beach is safe. They monitor the tides and weather, and look out for rip currents. When you are at the beach, you can ask the lifeguard to give you safety information. They respond to emergencies when a person is in danger in the water.

Some beaches do not have a lifeguard on duty, or a lifeguard may only be on duty during certain hours. You can check before you pick which beach to visit.

Beach Warning Flags

Public beaches often have a special flag system. Pay special attention to the flag systems on public beaches. A double red flag (see below) means the beach is closed. A red flag notes dangerous

 Water Closed to Public

 Low Hazard
Calm Conditions, Exercise Caution

 High Hazard
High Surf and/or Strong Currents

 Stinging/Hazardous Marine Life
Man o' War, Jellyfish, Stingrays

 Medium Hazard
Moderate Surf and/or Strong Currents

conditions due to strong currents or high surf. A yellow flag indicates a medium hazard (moderate conditions). A green flag is displayed when conditions are calm. A purple flag informs visitors that jellyfish or other dangerous marine life are present. When in doubt, ask lifeguards or other authorities for help.

Rip Currents

Rip currents, sometimes called *riptides*, can be dangerous and common, especially after storms. Put simply, a rip current is an area of current that moves away from the beach and into the ocean. Rip currents are essentially narrow channels of fast-moving water that can overtake even the best swimmers, dragging them into the open ocean. They often occur near structures such as piers or jetties, so don't swim near

them. If you're caught in a riptide, don't panic. Instead, signal/yell for help, and swim sideways (parallel) to the shore, not directly against the current. (Fighting a rip current would simply tire you out.) Rip currents are rarely more than 80 feet wide, so once you're free of the current, you should be able to turn and swim toward shore.

If you suspect someone's in trouble in the water, immediately notify a lifeguard and/or call 911.

Tsunamis

A *tsunami* is a large wave caused by an earthquake or volcanic activity. Tsunamis are an uncommon event on the Pacific Coast, and an even rarer event on the Atlantic Coast. Still, you should know what a tsunami is—and what to do in the super unlikely event one occurs. Large earthquakes, usually under the ocean, are the main causes of tsunamis. They can also be caused by volcanic activity and landslides. The force of the earthquakes, volcanic activity, or landslides cre-

ates a series of large waves that can flood beaches and travel far onto land.

When a tsunami is about to strike, water often pulls back from the beach first, exposing lots of sand and even shells and flopping fish. If this happens, you need to leave the beach and get to higher ground right away. Tsunami emergency signs often direct which way to go.

Weather agencies and governments may also signal a tsunami warning. As with other natural disasters, chances are you'll never experience a tsunami, but it's good to be prepared.

BEACH GEAR AND PRO TIPS

Sunscreen

Prepare for a visit by packing sunblock for protection from sunburn. You can also wear a hat, sunglasses, and long sleeves to protect your skin from the sun.

Water and Snacks

A day in the sun is hot, so it's important to pack water and snacks to keep you hydrated and fueled for a day of adventure.

Life Jackets/Swimming Safety

If you're swimming or going into the water, always have an adult with you or supervising, be sure to wear a life jacket/flotation device, and swim with at least one (or more) people. Your adult guardian may also consider carrying a water-rescue throw bag.

A Notebook and Binoculars

If you want to sketch your finds as you explore, a notebook is a great addition to a beach bag, and so are binoculars for spotting birds (and even boats/ships) from afar!

Collecting Rules and Etiquette

Check local beach rules to see if you are allowed to take shells home with you or if they should remain where you found them. Collecting shells that

Sanderling

are alive—with animals still inside them—is usually illegal, so leave them be! And before you collect any shells, smell them! Anything that smells fishy should stay at the beach.

Leave No Trace

The saying "leave no trace" means that when we visit a place, we leave it in as good a condition as we found it—or better! The goal is to leave only footprints behind. Our beaches are a treasure, so please do your best to take care of them.

Know Before You Go

Prepare for your visit by checking the rules for the beach. Take note of the weather forecast and any potential hazards. It's always a good idea to bring a map!

Choose the Right Path

Be sure to walk along maintained trails. Sand dunes are especially vulnerable, so please stay off them and stick to boardwalks and paved trails instead.

Respect the Wildlife

We share beaches with a variety of wildlife; whenever possible, simply admire beach life from a distance. When you visit the beach, be respectful of the wildlife. Don't chase birds or get too close to animals.

Leave What You Find

Close observation, photographs, or drawings are great ways to remember what you saw at the beach. The things you discover at the beach belong right where you find them. Leave those discoveries behind to protect nature and so other visitors can enjoy them too. If you do decide to take shells home, make sure you leave anything still living right where you found it, and check local beach rules to confirm whether taking shells home is allowed.

Properly Dispose of Trash

Make sure you place any trash and recyclables in the proper bins. If bins are not available, take these items home with you. Trash can harm or even kill wildlife.

Be Careful with Fire

Campfires can be dangerous and hurt the environment, wildlife, and other people. If the beach you're visiting allows fires, use established fire rings. Before you leave, make sure you put out the fire completely.

Be Kind to Other Visitors

All the visitors at the beach—including you!—are excited to enjoy their day exploring, playing and relaxing. Be courteous and respectful of other visitors so everybody can have a good experience. A little kindness goes a long way.

How to Use This Book

This book is intended to help you identify the animals and other life-forms you see at the beach. Because North America's beaches differ a lot, depending on whether you're on the Atlantic Coast of Florida or the rocky Pacific Coast of Washington State, this book is split into two main parts. One field guide, starting on page 46, covers the beach life and animals you'll find on the Atlantic and Gulf Coast. The field guide for the Pacific Coast starts on page 80.

Within each section, the animals and plants are organized in groups—birds, shells, and so on—with photos to help you identify common beach finds.

But before you dive in there, it's helpful to take a look at the bigger picture. Here's a quick rundown of both our coasts and how they form, as well as maps showing some famous beaches, seashores, and other sites, such as areas with tidepools.

Ochre sea stars

The Atlantic and Gulf Coasts
NOTABLE BEACHES

Galveston, TX

Holly Beach, LA

Grand Isle Beach, LA

Biloxi, MS

Gulf Islands National Seashore, MS

Orange Beach, AL

Pensacola Beach, FL

Destin, FL

Tampa, FL

St. Petersburg, FL

Fort Myers, FL

Naples, FL

Miami Beach, FL

Cape Canaveral National Seashore, FL

Daytona Beach, FL

Amelia Island, FL

Cumberland Island National Seashore, GA

Tybee Island, GA

Hilton Head, SC

Folly Beach, SC

Myrtle Beach, SC

Outer Banks, NC

Virginia Beach, VA

Rehoboth Beach, DE

25 Asbury Park on the Jersey Shore, NJ

26 Fire Island, NY

27 Hampton Beach, NY

28 Montauk, NY

29 Martha's Vineyard, MA

30 Cape Cod, MA

31 Old Orchard, ME

32 Acadia National Park, ME

HOW BEACHES FORMED ON THE GULF AND ATLANTIC COASTS

Ocean levels have risen and fallen and risen and fallen many times since the Earth formed about 4.5 billion years ago. The history of the Atlantic Ocean begins 150 million years ago. Back then, all of our current continents formed one super-continent, known as Pangaea. When the movement of large, underground pieces of Earth's crust—known as *plates*—started to fracture under Pangaea, a brand new crust appeared far below the surface of the ocean in what we now call the Mid-Atlantic Ridge. As Pangaea broke up into different continents, they in turn continued to move farther apart (just a few centimeters each year, which is why you can't feel this movement). As they moved into their current locations, the Atlantic Ocean formed in between. The formation of the Atlantic Ocean is the beginning of the stories of our coastal beaches here.

Florida: Much of Florida's east coast is flanked by barrier islands. During the end of the last ice age, about 18,000 years ago, the ocean was 360 feet *lower* than it is today. Rivers brought sediment, like soil and rocks, out to the ocean, where it piled up to form ridges and dunes. When sea levels eventually rose as the glaciers melted, the water moved into the low-lying areas behind the ridges, creating barrier islands. Now surrounded by water, sand accumulated on these islands to form beaches.

The Gulf of Mexico: Many Gulf of Mexico beaches, especially in Florida and Alabama, are known for their fine, white "sugar sand." This sugar sand is actually made up of tiny pieces of quartz that have washed down from the Appalachian Mountains through inland rivers, which eventually flow into the Gulf of Mexico. Gulf currents sweep the sand onto the beaches.

North Carolina: The coastal shelf—a relatively shallow area of water at the edge of a continent that is often exposed when sea level rise declines, then gets submerged again as sea levels go up—gradually extends downward into the sea. Tides in the North Carolina area are less than 10 feet of difference each day, but that is enough to bring more sand and material to the shoreline, allowing barrier islands to form in what is now known as the Outer Banks. These islands also sport sandy beaches and unique habitat for birds and sea turtles.

Mid-Atlantic: The current beaches and barrier islands of Delaware, Maryland, and Virginia formed as mountains farther inland eroded, providing sediment that eventually became the sand found on the coasts. In one area, so much sediment has eroded from the Appalachian Mountain range that these peaks are now 100 miles from the coastline! At the same time, sand ridges left over from earlier ocean levels provide the sand that eventually collects on our beaches. Sand is kept here through a variety of forces, including wind and regular tides.

The Appalachian Mountains were originally as tall as the Rockies.

EROSION

The shoreline today

The Appalachian Mountains today

Bedrock

New York and New England:

North of New York, the coast changes. Thousands of years ago, giant glaciers used to sit here, and when they melted, they quite literally scraped away all the soil and sediment that had been accumulating over time, moving into giant piles (known as *moraines*) in what is now Nantucket, Cape Cod, Long Island, and Martha's Vineyard. Sand built up along the coast to become the beaches we know today, many of which have steep, rocky cliffs (especially in Maine).

A barrier island offshore

Continental shelf

Shelf

Atlantic Ocean

The Pacific Coast
NOTABLE BEACHES

Cabrillo National Monument, CA

La Jolla Cove, CA

Dana Strands Beach, CA

White Point Beach, CA

Carrillo State Beach, CA

Montaña de Oro State Park, CA

Big Sur, CA

Natural Bridges State Park, CA

Pebble Beach, CA

Mendocino Headlands, CA

MacKerricher State Park, CA

Port Orford, OR

Shore Acres State Park, OR

Agate Beach, OR

Yaquina Head, OR

Hug Point, OR

Canon Beach and Haystack Rock, OR

Ecola State Park, OR

Cape Disappointment State Park, WA

Ruby Beach, WA

Rialto Beach, WA

Hole-in-the-Wall Beach, WA

Salt Creek Recreation Area, WA

Alki Beach, WA

HOW BEACHES FORMED ON THE PACIFIC COAST

Over millions of years, the Pacific Coast was created by strong natural forces. Many of its characteristic features are the products of geologic activity (including volcanic activity) and erosion by exposure to wind and water.

Plate Tectonics: Plate tectonics is the scientific theory that describes how the earth's crust is made of multiple large plates that are always moving. The largest of these plates is the Pacific Plate, followed by the North American Plate. The outer edge of the Pacific Plate, dubbed the Ring of Fire, is well known for volcanic activity. 75% of the world's active volcanoes are located on the Ring of Fire. Major changes to the earth's crust occur where two or more tectonic plates collide, move away from each other, or slide past each other. The movement and interaction between plates create mountain ranges, new land, trenches, volcanoes, earthquakes, and tsunamis.

The Pacific Coast is affected primarily by interactions between the Pacific Plate and North American Plate. A smaller plate called the Juan de Fuca Plate sits between the two major plates to the west of Washington and Oregon.

Geologic Uplift: Along the Pacific Coast, one outcome of the tectonic plates colliding is *uplift,* which means land is pushed upward. The upward movement

can be uneven, resulting in a tilt. At many beaches, you can see layers in the rock that are no longer horizontal as they were formed.

Arches, Cliffs, and Sea Stacks:

As geologic uplift happens and land rises out of the ocean, the ocean currents and wave action continue to sculpt this land, eroding away fractured and softer rock. The rock that is more resistant to erosion remains as dramatic cliffs, arches, and sea stacks.

Tidepools: Abundant rocky shores are another product of the geologic activity that has shaped the Pacific Coast. Where there are depressions in the rock in the Intertidal Zone, water is trapped as the ocean recedes during low tide. Many species are specially adapted to thrive in this challenging habitat.

Sandy Beaches: The loose sediment that makes up sandy beaches on the Pacific Coast travels from the mountain ranges. Sediment weathers and becomes finer as it travels along waterways from mountains to shore. Compared to the Atlantic Coast, the mountain ranges are very close to the shore, and therefore the sediment on the Pacific Coast is coarser because it does not undergo as much weathering.

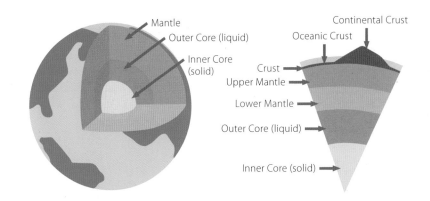

Atlantic and Gulf Field Guide

SHELLS

There are hundreds of shells that wash up on Atlantic Ocean beaches, but some are more common than others. Remember: if there is a living creature within the shell, throw it back! Check local beach rules to see if you are allowed to take shells home with you, or if they should remain where you found them.

There are several kinds of animals with shells, including bivalves, sea urchins, gastropods (like snails and slugs), and more!

The best times of the year for shelling are in the spring and during low tide. However, shelling is also excellent after major storms have moved shells from farther offshore up onto the beaches, which can occur from late spring all the way until the end of November. What will you find?

Bivalves

These creatures live inside a shell that has two parts, coming together in a hinge. They can live in both fresh and salt water.

Turkey Wing Shell
Arca zebra

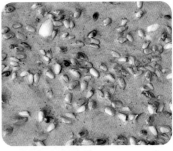

Coquina Shell
Donax variabilis

Calico Scallop
Argopecten gibbus

Oyster Shell
Crassostrea virginica

Atlantic Jackknife Clam
Ensis leei

Southern Quahog
Mercenaria campechiensis

Mussel
Mytilus edulis

Iceland Scallop
Chlamys islandica

Atlantic Surf Clam
Spisula solidissima

Cockle Shell
Cardiidae (family)

Jingle Shell
Anomia simplex

Echinododerms

The name *echinoderm* means "spiny skin," which is a key characteristic of these kinds of animals. Echinoderms are also well known for their radial symmetry (which means their shape has a pattern that repeats around a center, like a star) and tube feet, which act as little suction cups to hold on to surfaces and also help move food to the mouth.

Brittle Star
Ophiopholis aculeata

Sea Urchin
Echinoidea (class)

Sand Dollar
Echinarachnius parma

Gastropods

Also known as snails, whelks, and slugs, gastropods have no shell or just a univalve shell, and are known for the sensory organs sticking right out of their heads!

Lightning Whelk Shell
Sinistrofulgur perversum

Limpets
Patellogastropoda (order)

Marsh Periwinkle
Littoraria irrorata

Atlantic Slipper Shells
Crepidula fornicata

Whelk Egg Case

Augers
Terebridae (family)

Conch Shell
Fasciolariidae (family)

Junonia Shell
Scaphella junonia

Tulip-Banded Shell
Cinctura (genus)

Murex Shell
Muricidae (family)

Cerith Shell
Cerithium (family)

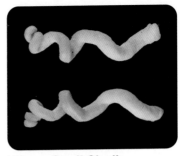

Worm Snail Shells
Vermetidae (family)

New England Neptune
Neptunea lyrata

CORAL

Coral reefs form in the Atlantic waters of Florida; in fact, Florida's reefs are the third-largest barrier reef system on Earth. The majority of these reefs lie within Biscayne Bay National Park and the Florida Keys National Marine Sanctuary. Some of the most common coral species present are shown below.

Boulder Star
Montastrea annularis

Great Star
Montastrea cavernosa

Massive Starlet
Siderastrea siderea

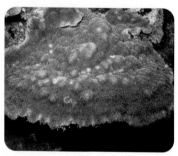

Mustard Hill
Porites astroides

Grooved Brain
Colpophyllia natans

Coral Piece

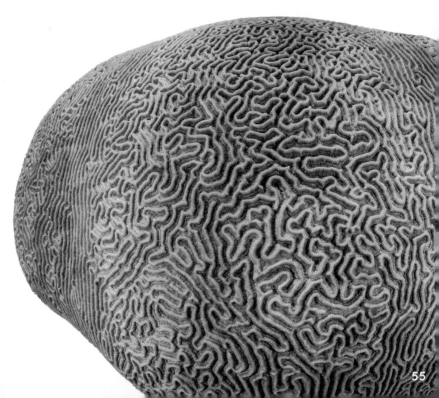

SEA TURTLES

All sea turtles along the Atlantic Ocean and Gulf of Mexico are listed as endangered or threatened species, but they are making a comeback. Thanks to nonprofit and government efforts to protect their nests, sea turtle nests are on the rebound.

Sea turtles swim offshore as they feed, and during the summer months they haul themselves onto the beach during the night to dig holes with powerful flippers before depositing golf ball-sized eggs. The baby turtles hatch during the night as well, using light reflected off the waves to guide them back to the sea. If you see an adult, a baby turtle, or an egg, don't touch them! Interfering with them in any way is illegal.

Do you live along the beach? Turn out your lights! Both adult and baby sea turtles can mistake house lights for the moon and stars, causing them to move in the wrong direction. Turn off your lights at night, or replace them with amber-colored bulbs to help sea turtles in your area have a successful nesting season.

Loggerhead Sea Turtle
Caretta caretta

Green Sea Turtle
Chelonia mydas

Leatherback Sea Turtle
Dermochelys coriacea

Kemp's Ridley Sea Turtle
Lepidochelys kempii

Hawksbill Sea Turtle
Eretmochelys imbricata

This turtle is pictured with a tracking device, which helps scientists learn more about this rare creature!

BIRDS

Beaches host year-round avian residents, summer breeders, migratory visitors, and winter resters. In fact, you can identify the season by identifying which birds flock to the beaches! To find beach birds, look for their silhouettes along three different zones: 1) in the sky, soaring overhead; 2) running along or standing on the beach itself; 3) floating on the waves offshore. Different species will use different areas as they rest, search for food, and raise their young.

Do you see bands on the birds' legs? Great! These bands provide important information for researchers studying these species. Note the colors of the bands or take a picture, then report your sighting at www.reportband.gov.

Birds are best seen through binoculars or in a camera lens. Avoid spooking or scaring the birds: if they run or fly away (*flush*), the birds expend critical energy they need for finding food, and this can leave chicks or eggs vulnerable to the heat or predators. Give the birds their space, and do not feed them. The birds listed on the following pages are among the more common species found on our Atlantic beaches.

Gulls

Herring Gull
Larus argentatus

Laughing Gull
Leucophaeus atricilla

Ring-Billed Gull
Larus delawarensis

Bonaparte's Gull
Chroicocephalus philadelphia

Great Black-Backed Gull
Larus marinus

Nonbreeding Bonaparte's Gulls are more likely in the winter. Pictured here is a gull in nonbreeding plumage.

Raptors

Osprey
Pandion haliaetus

Bald Eagle
Haliaeetus leucocephalus

Terns

Least Tern
Sternula antillarum

Royal Tern
Thalasseus maximus

Sandwich Tern
Thalasseus sandvicensis

Caspian Tern
Hydroprogne caspia

Common Tern
Sterna hirundo

nonbreeding plumage

Forster's Tern
Sterna forsteri

Roseate Tern
Sterna dougallii

Seabirds

Brown Pelican
Pelecanus occidentalis

nonbreeding plumage

Common Loon
Gavia immer

nonbreeding plumage

Horned Grebe
Podiceps auritus

Red-Breasted Merganser
Mergus serrator

Usually seen in spring, summer, and fall

Double-Crested Cormorant
Nannopterum auritum

Usually seen in winter

Great Cormorant
Phalacrocorax carbo

Long-Tailed Duck
Clangula hyemalis

Common Eider
Somateria mollissima

Seabirds

Common Goldeneye
Bucephala clangula

Wading

Great Blue Heron
Ardea herodias

Tricolored Heron
Egretta tricolor

Great Egret
Ardea alba

Snowy Egret
Egretta thula

Shorebirds

Sanderling
Calidris alba

Willet
Tringa semipalmata

Ruddy Turnstone
Arenaria interpres

Wilson's Plover
Charadrius wilsonia

Seen in winter

Purple Sandpiper
Calidris maritima

Dunlin
Calidris alpina

ICONIC CREATURES

So much of what you can spot on the beach is small, from tiny seashells to delicate flowers to hand-sized shorebirds. But beaches can be home to big creatures as well. Here are some of the most well known!

Manatee

Manatees are mammals, and they can be spotted along the Gulf of Mexico or Atlantic Ocean when they are on the move between seasons. Though they are large, they are very gentle, eating only grasses and vegetation.

Manatee
Trichechus manatus latirostris

Alligator
Alligator mississippiensis

Alligator

Wait, alligators can swim in the ocean? Yes! Though it is less common, American Alligators can use water routes near beaches and bays to move from one freshwater habitat to another.

Seals

Seals are water-loving mammals that don't mind the cold! Look for their heads jutting just above the water in harbors and near beaches.

Harbor Seals
Phoca vitulina

Gray Seal
Halichoerus grypus

Whales and Dolphins

If you're lucky, you can spot whales from the beaches when they come in close to shore.

Humpback Whale
Megaptera novaeangliae

North Atlantic Right Whale
Eubalaena glacialis

We love dolphins! They often feed in the waves near shore, and they can be spotted as they surface to breathe or when they jump into the air.

Common Bottlenose Dolphin
Tursiops truncatus

FISH

You can find many fish species living in the different beach habitats. Some fish live in deeper waters and can be seen when they are commonly caught at fishing piers (that rent fishing gear!), while other fish can be admired in tidepools. Some fish swimming in shallow water can even be seen from shore.

Pompano
Trachinotus (genus)

Redfish
Sciaenops ocellatus

Tarpon
Megalops atlanticus

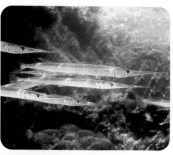

Needlefish
Belonidae (family)

Mullet
Mugil cephalus

Spanish Mackerel
Scomberomorus maculatus

Ladyfish
Elops saurus

Spotted Sea Trout
Cynoscion nebulosus

Atlantic Mackerel
Scomber scombrus

Striped Bass
Morone saxatilis

SHARKS

It's true, there are a lot of sharks in our waters, but negative interactions with sharks are incredibly rare. In fact, sharks are pretty good neighbors most of the time. They play an important role in nearshore, offshore, and reef ecosystems, acting as the apex (top) predator. To stay extra-safe, swim where there are lifeguards present, exit the water if a shark has been spotted, and do not harass a shark in any way. Looking to find shark's teeth? Venice Beach, Florida, is known for its shark teeth, as are the beaches around Jacksonville and Topsail Beach in North Carolina, and Folly Beach in South Carolina.

Great Hammerhead Shark
Sphyrna mokarran

Tiger Shark
Galeocerdo cuvier

Scalloped Hammerhead
Sphyrna lewini

Bull Shark
Carcharhinus leucas

Great White Shark
Carcharodon carcharias

Lemon Shark
Negaprion brevirostris

Sandbar Shark
Carcharhinus plumbeus

Reef Shark (Florida Keys)
Carcharhinus perezi

Blacktip Shark
Carcharhinus limbatus

Dusky Shark
Carcharhinus obscurus

**Atlantic Spiny
Dogfish Shark**
Squalus acanthias

**Atlantic Sharpnose
Shark**
Rhizoprionodon terraenovae

JELLYFISH AND JELLYFISH-LIKE CRITTERS

Don't touch! They may be beautiful, but avoid touching jellyfish. Some species have very long tentacles that can be nearly invisible, so give jellyfish lots of space in order to avoid a sting.

Did you know? Only 5 percent of a jellyfish is actual body mass: the rest is water. Jellyfish are critical food sources for sea turtles!

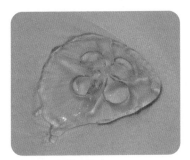

Moon Jellyfish
Aurelia aurita

Cannonball Jellyfish
Stomolophus meleagris

Portuguese Man-o-War
Physalia physalis

Sea Nettle Jellyfish
Chrysaora quinquecirrha

Lion's Mane Jellyfish
Cyanea capillata

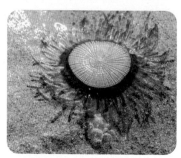

Blue Button Jellyfish
Porpita Porpita

By-the-Wind Sailor Jellyfish
Velella velella

Mushroom Cap Jellyfish
Rhopilema verrilli

Sea Walnut
Mnemiopsis leidyi

Pink Cone Jellyfish
Beroe ovata

CRUSTACEANS

Look along most expanses of beach and you should be able to spot a crab species. From the Ghost Crabs that skitter along the sand to the sand fleas that burrow in it to the varieties found just offshore, crabs are a common sight along our Gulf of Mexico and Atlantic Ocean beaches.

Ghost Crab
Ocypode quadrata

Blue Crab
Callinectes sapidus

Lobster
Homarus americanus

Sand Flea
Emerita (genus)

Atlantic Rock Crab
Cancer irroratus

Fiddler Crab
Uca pugilator

Purple Marsh Crab
Sesarma reticulatum

Jonah Crab
Cancer borealis

Horseshoe Crab
Limulus polyphemus

While these may look like crab relatives, they are actually more closely related to spiders.

ANEMONES

They may look like flowering plants, but anenomes are actually predatory animals!

North American Tube-Dwelling Anemone
Ceriantheopsis americana

SEAWEED AND PLANTS

Aquatic plants, including both those growing in the shallows and washed up on the beach, provide critical habitat and nutrients in this otherwise sandy environment. Similarly, plants growing along the dunes stabilize these sandforms and protect the interior of the coast from storms and surges.

Sea oats grow on the coast of Florida all the way up through Virginia. Their roots stabilize the dunes and create habitat for a variety of species.

Sea Oats
Uniola paniculata

Sargassum seaweed
Sargassaceae (family)

Pushed to beaches by the Gulf Stream, this particular species of seaweed can wash ashore in the tons.

Rockweed
Ascophyllum nodosum

Sea bean (aka drift seed)
(Various species)

As its name implies, this seaweed grows along the rocks of beaches or near the high-tide line (depending on the subspecies).

SEAGLASS

Beachcombing is a popular activity because you can find little pieces of history hidden within the sand: seaglass!

Salt water and sand smooth the sharp edges of glass fragments, making them safe to handle as well as beautiful. Brown, green, and white are the most common colors, while blue, red, and purple are harder to come by.

Did you know? Orange is the rarest seaglass hue.

Looking to visit a beach in hopes of discovering seaglass? Florida has more seaglass than any other state. Florida's Hutchinson Island is well known for its seaglass!

Pacific Field Guide

SHELLS

Shells are fun to explore at the beach and provide clues to understand what animals live nearby. High tides push shells onto shore, and the best time to look for shells is during low tide, when it's easy to access more areas of the beach. Remember: if there is a living creature within the shell, put it back! Check local beach rules to see if you are allowed to take shells home with you or if they should remain where you found them.

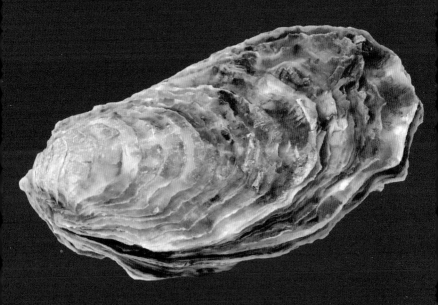

Gastropods

The word *gastropod* means "stomach foot," which describes the flat part of the body that these animals use to crawl along surfaces. Snails and slugs are gastropods. Some gastropods have a shell, as snails do.

Rough Keyhole Limpet
Diodora aspera

Shield Limpet
Lottia pelta

Striped Dogwinkle
Nucella ostrina

Black Turban Shell
Tegula funebralis

Checkered Periwinkle
Littorina scutulata

Eroded Periwinkle
Littorina keenae

Bivalves

Bivalves are animals that have two parts to the shell that are kept shut by a strong muscle. They have a siphon (shaped like a tube) that they reach out of the shell to filter their food.

Razor Clam
Siliqua patula

Blue Mussel
Mytilus edulis

Olympia Oyster
Ostrea lurida

This is the only oyster species that is native to the Pacific Coast of North America. People have brought many other oyster species to be farmed.

Echinoderms

The name *echinoderm* means "spiny skin," which is a key characteristic of these kinds of animals. Echinoderms are also well known for their radial symmetry (which means their shape has a pattern that repeats around a center, like a star) and tube feet, which act as little suction cups to hold on to surfaces and also help move food to the mouth.

Pacific Sand Dollar
Dendraster excentricus

Purple Sea Urchin
Strongylocentrotus purpuratus

Red Sea Urchin
Mesocentrotus franciscanus

The shells of different sea urchin species look very similar and can be difficult to tell apart.

Ochre Sea Star
Pisaster ochraceus

Bat Star
Patiria miniata

SEAGLASS

As you explore the beach, you may notice seaglass. These are glass fragments that have been polished by the movement of salt water and sand, making them safe to handle. While glass can form naturally, a lot of the seaglass you find contains little pieces of human history. For example, Glass Beach in Fort Bragg, California, is well known for its seaglass and was formerly a dump site for trash. The seaglass you find there today is made from broken glass bottles. One person's trash becomes another person's treasure!

In Oregon, you may find a rare glass float. Long ago, fishermen would use hollow glass spheres to keep their nets afloat. Nowadays, fishing floats are made of plastic. There are many glass floats stuck out in the Pacific Ocean, but sometimes a shift in the currents will move some of the floats to the Oregon shoreline. In Lincoln City, Oregon, glass artists make new glass floats, and volunteers hide them on the beach for beachcombers to find and take home.

Glass at Glass Beach
Fort Bragg, California

Oregon glass floats

Seaglass on the Pacific Coast

ANEMONES

Anemones are invertebrates (animals without bones) with tentacles for stinging their prey (like small crabs and fish). An anemone also uses tentacles to move food to its mouth. During low tide, anemones pull in their tentacles and fold their bodies inward to survive exposure to the air.

Giant Green Anemone
Anthopleura xanthogrammica

Aggregating Anemone
Anthopleura elegantissima

JELLYFISH AND JELLYFISH-LIKE CREATURES

Jellyfish live entirely in the ocean, but you can find jellyfish in shallow waters and sometimes see them washed up on shore. Be on the lookout for them while swimming and exploring the beach. While they are fun to spot, they can sting in the water, and they can still sting after they have washed ashore. On shore, it can sometimes be difficult to see all of a jellyfish's tentacles, so keep your distance!

By-the-Wind Sailor
Velella velella

West Coast Sea Nettle
Chrysaora fuscescens

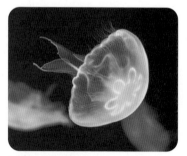

Moon Jelly
Aurelia aurita

Purple-Striped Jelly
Chrysaora colorata

CRUSTACEANS

Crustaceans are animals with segmented bodies and an exoskeleton (an outer skeleton) instead of bones. Beware of the claws or pincers on the front legs of crabs. They can deliver a strong pinch!

Striped Shore Crab
Pachygrapsus crassipes

Purple Shore Crab
Hemigrapsus nudus

Blue-Banded Hermit Crab
Pagurus samuelis

Grainy Hermit Crab
Pagurus granosimanus

This species' sting can hurt. Keep your distance from the tentacles of this one.

Kelp Crab
Pugettia producta

Crabs aren't the only crustaceans out there. Mole crabs live shallowly buried in the sand, while barnacles attach themselves to rocks or even whales.

Pacific Mole Crab
Emerita analoga

Gooseneck Barnacle
Pollicipes polymerus

Pink Volcano Barnacle
Tetraclita rubescens

CORAL

While corals look like rocks, they are living, growing animals! These tiny animals attach themselves to something hard, like a rock, for protection. Corals have soft bodies, and some grow a hard exoskeleton for protection.

California Hydrocoral
Stylaster californicus

Red Gorgonian
Lophogorgia chilensis

FISH

You can find many fish species living in the different beach habitats. Some fish live in deeper waters and can be seen when they are commonly caught at fishing piers, while other fish can be admired in tidepools. Some fish swimming in shallow water can even be seen from shore.

Garibaldi
Hypsypops rubicundus

California Sheephead
Semicossyphus pulcher

Opaleye
Girella nigricans

Lingcod
Ophiodon elongatus

Cabezon
Scorpaenichthys marmoratus

Blue Rockfish
Sebastes mystinus

Redtail Surfperch
Amphistichus rhodoterus

Striped Bass
Morone saxatilis

Pink Salmon
Oncorhynchus gorbuscha

Starry Flounder
Platichthys stellatus

Pacific Halibut
Hippoglossus stenolepis

Garibaldi

SHARKS AND RAYS

Sharks and rays are cartilaginous fish, which means that they have skeletons made mostly of cartilage, not bone. Rays can be seen swimming at the surface or jumping out of the water, and some sharks can be viewed by looking into the water from higher vantage points. Safety tip: Some rays rest in the sand in shallow water; you can reduce your risk of stepping on a ray by shuffling your feet in the sand as you walk. Even though there is a lot of attention paid to shark attacks, they are very rare events. At the beach, you can ask the lifeguard if there have been any recent shark sightings.

Bat Ray
Myliobatis californica

Round Stingray
Urolophus halleri

Leopard Shark
Triakis semifasciata

Great White Shark
Carcharodon carcharias

BIRDS

Beaches host year-round avian residents, summer breeders, migratory visitors, and winter resters. Different species will utilize different areas as they rest, search for food, and raise their young. To find beach birds, look for their silhouettes along three different planes: 1) in the sky, soaring overhead; 2) running along or standing on the beach itself; 3) floating on the waves offshore. The coastal marshes are a great place to look for birds because this habitat is very important for the birds that migrate. The marshes are like stepping stones helping birds fly north and south on the migratory route known as the Pacific Flyway. Birds stop in marshes and other habitats along the way to rest and replenish themselves with food. A good time to look for birds is during peak migration, which happens twice per year. Peak fall migration lasts from mid-August to mid-October, while peak spring migration is shorter, from mid-March to mid-April.

Do you see bands on the birds' legs? Great! These bands provide important information for researchers studying these species. Note the colors of the bands or take a picture, then report your sighting here at www.reportband.gov.

Birds are best seen through binoculars or in a camera lens. Avoid spooking or scaring the birds—if they flush, the birds expend critical energy they need for finding food and can leave chicks or eggs vulnerable to the heat or predators. Give the birds their space, and do not feed them. These are not all the possible birds you can spot on the beach, but they do include the more common species.

Gulls

California Gull
Larus californicus

Ring-Billed Gull
Larus delawarensis

Glaucous-Winged Gull
Larus glaucescens

Herring Gull
Larus argentatus

The word *glaucous* means dull gray or blue.

Heermann's Gull
Larus heermanni

Western Gull
Larus occidentalis

Terns

Caspian Tern
Hydroprogne caspia

Common Tern
Sterna hirundo

nonbreeding
plumage

Forster's Tern
Sterna forsteri

Seabirds

Double-Crested Cormorant
Nannopterum auritum

Brandt's Cormorant
Urile penicillatus

Brown Pelican
Pelecanus occidentalis

nonbreeding plumage

Common Loon
Gavia immer

nonbreeding plumage

Horned Grebe
Podiceps auritus

Red-Breasted Merganser
Mergus serrator

Raptors

Northern Harrier
Circus hudsonius

Osprey
Pandion haliaetus

Bald Eagle
Haliaeetus leucocephalus

Shorebirds

Western Sandpiper
Calidris mauri

Marbled Godwit
Limosa fedoa

Killdeer
Charadrius vociferus

Sanderling
Calidris alba

Willet
Tringa semipalmata

Ruddy Turnstone
Arenaria interpres

Black Turnstone
Arenaria melanocephala

Black Oystercatcher
Haematopus bachmani

Ducks

For many duck species, individuals look different if they are male or female. Males tend to have plumage (feathers) that are more brightly colored or more boldly patterned. Females tend to have brown and tan plumage, without bold patterns.

Surf Scoter (male)
Melanitta perspicillata

Surf Scoter (female)

American Wigeon
Mareca americana

Northern Pintail
Anas acuta

Bufflehead
Bucephala albeola

American Avocet
Recurvirostra americana

Great Blue Heron
Ardea herodias

Great Egret
Ardea alba

Snowy Egret
Egretta thula

Black-Necked Stilt
Himantopus mexicanus

Great Blue Heron

MAMMALS

Otters

Otters are carnivorous mammals. Sea otters live in nearshore ocean waters and can live their entire life without leaving the water. River otters are semiaquatic, and in addition to living on rivers, they can also be seen foraging in the waters offshore, in estuaries, and in marshes.

Sea Otter
Enhydra lutris

River Otter
Lontra canadensis

Pinnipeds (Seals and Sea Lions)

Pinnipeds have front and rear flippers instead of feet. They forage in the ocean and drag themselves on land to rest and reproduce. These animals are large and will defend themselves and their young from people who get too close. When you find them at the beach, it is best to observe them from a distance. In fact, at Año Nuevo State Park in California, you must book a tour with a docent to be able to see the Northern Elephant Seals.

California Sea Lion
Zalophus californianus

Steller Sea Lion (male)
Eumetopias jubatus

Northern Elephant Seal
Mirounga angustirostris

Northern Fur Seal
Callorhinus ursinus

Harbor Seal
Phoca vitulina

Whales and Dolphins

If you're lucky, you can spot whales and dolphins from the beaches when they come in close to shore. Dolphins can sometimes be seen playing in the waves. Whales might be spotted as they migrate north and south along the Pacific Coast. Search from a higher vantage point (like atop a coastal bluff) to search for whale spouts farther out in the open ocean.

Common Bottlenose Dolphin
Tursiops truncatus

Orca
Orcinus orca

Gray Whale
Eschrichtius robustus

SEA TURTLES

It is very rare to see a sea turtle on the Pacific Coast, but they are very special visitors. Some of them travel all the way from the other side of the Pacific Ocean to eat jellyfish, then journey back across the ocean. All species of sea turtle that visit the Pacific Coast are threatened or endangered.

This turtle has a GPS tag on its back to track its location in the wild. It was rescued, recovered in captivity, and released back into the Pacific Ocean.

Olive Ridley Sea Turtle
Lepidochelys olivacea

Green Sea Turtle
Chelonia mydas

Leatherback Sea Turtle
Dermochelys coriacea

Loggerhead Sea Turtles
Caretta caretta

SEAWEED AND PLANTS

There are many species of plants that live on land in the different beach habitats, and many more plants that live in the water. Just like plants on land, marine plants and seaweeds create the habitat that animal species depend on. They support the entire food web in their ecosystem. You can see them in the intertidal zone and washed up in the wrack line.

Even though seaweeds like kelp look like plants, they are actually marine algae. The part that looks like roots is called a *holdfast* and keeps the seaweed anchored to the ocean floor or the surfaces of the rocky shore.

Terrestrial Plants (Plants on Land)

Pink Sand Verbena
Abronia umbellata

Beach Strawberry
Fragaria chiloensis

Marine Plants

Surfgrass
Phyllospadix (genus)

Seaweeds (Marine Algae)

Studded Sea Balloon
Soranthera ulvoidea

Red Coralline Algae
Calliarthron spp.

Rockweed
Fucus vesiculosus

Giant Kelp
Macrocystis pyrifera

Sea Palm
Postelsia palmaeformis

Kelp forest

Beach Activities

ACTIVITY: BEACH CLEANUP

Beach Debris

Currents and tides bring a variety of human-made objects to our shores, both from the recent past as well as history. Have you seen people walking the beaches with a long metal pole attached to a disk? That's a metal detector! Metal detectors help people find metal objects—like rings or coins—even if they are buried in the sand. But you can find cool objects even without a metal detector, just keep your eyes peeled!

Did you know? In 1992, a large cargo ship container carrying 28,000 rubber ducks fell into the ocean, sweeping all the rubber ducks into the sea. These rubber ducks washed ashore all over the world, from Maine to Australia, Alaska to the Arctic. You never know what you'll find on the beach!

Note: If you are looking for historic items beneath the water, you may need a special permit.

Beach Cleanup

Unfortunately, you can find some not-so-cool items, like trash or litter. Plastic pollution on beaches and in the ocean is a big and growing problem. When plastic items (for example plastic bottles, shopping bags, fishing line, to-go containers, and cigarette butts) are not discarded properly, they can make it difficult for wildlife to use the habitat for foraging, resting, and reproducing. Sometimes wildlife end up eating the plastic, and because it can't be digested, the plastic can make animals sick and die.

Take a bag with you to the beach to pick up these left items so you can properly dispose of them later and leave the beach cleaner than you found it! You can do this on your own, or join a beach cleanup event with other volunteers. Many organizations organize beach cleanups to make the habitat accessible and safe for the animals that need it and for the people who enjoy it too. Check out your local coastal- and ocean-advocacy groups to get involved with year-round beach cleanups or International Coastal Cleanup Day.

ACTIVITY: GO TIDEPOOLING

During low tide, the ocean recedes from the land and exposes tidepools. Tidepools are often thought of as depressions in the rock on rocky shores, in which water and sea life are trapped until high tide returns. Some tidepools are not in rock at all but are depressions in the sand that hold water during low tide. Tidepools are sort of like "mini oceans," and they are a great spot to explore and learn about the ocean.

What You Need
- Closed-toe shoes
- A tide table for the beach you're visiting
- A camera or notebook (optional)
- A field guide (optional)

The first step to exploring a tidepool is finding one. The Pacific Coast is more well known for its tidepools than the Atlantic Coast, but both coasts have plenty of places to explore tidepools.

TIDEPOOL LIFE

Nudibranchs: Nudibranchs (
special animals to find. You'll
on seaweed or rocks. They c
ter of an inch, but some can
In tidepools, you will probably
so look carefully. There are a
nudibranch off the Pacific Co
related to snails and slugs bu
Most nudibranchs get their c

Opalescent Nudibranch
Hermissenda opalescens

Gray Sea Slug
Aeolidia papillosa

TIDEPOOLS ON THE PACIFIC COAST

1 La Jolla Cove, California

2 Montaña de Oro State Park, California

3 Yaquina Head Outstanding Natural Area, Oregon

4 Cannon Beach, Oregon

5 Shi Shi Beach, Olympic National Park, Washington

6 Salt Creek Recreation Area, Washington

7 Alki Beach Park, Washington

TIDEPOOLS ON THE ATLANTIC COAST

1 Bahia Honda State Park, Florida

2 Tybee Island, Georgia

3 Hunting Island State Park, South Carolina

4 First Encounter Beach, Massachusetts

5 Old Orchard Beach, Maine

6 Wonderland Trail, Acadia National Park, Maine

After you've narrowed dow
explore, you need to check
tidepools are under water
to time your visit right. Bef
sure you've got good shoes
slippery. Tall rubber boots

Once you arrive at the tide
things to keep in mind to ke
in the tidepools safe while y
face the ocean and keep an
turn your back on the ocea
an unusually large wave (aka
catch you by surprise. Resp
by stepping carefully aroun
gently (when it's safe to do
up to take a closer look, put
it. If you pick up a rock to se
the rock carefully back dow
creatures down beside the
way around. Remember, if y
up, and it doesn't budge, lea

There are lots of creatures
tidepools. To survive being
during low tide, animals like
rocks and mussels stay tight
pools, you can often find sea
sculpins and other small fish
stars come in many shapes,

Chitons: Chitons (pronounced "kite-on") are also a kind of gastropod that has eight shell plates that slightly overlap. They use their muscular foot to hold onto rocks in the intertidal zone.

Eastern Beaded Chiton
Chaetopleura apiculata

Mossy Chiton
Mopalia muscosa

Black Leather Chiton
Katharina tunicata

Woolly Sculpin
Clinocottus analis

Grunt Sculpin
Rhamphocottus richardsonii

Black Turban Snail
Tegula funebralis

Ochre Sea Star
Pisaster ochraceus

Bat Star
Patiria miniata

Common Sea Star
Asterias rubens

Forbes's Sea Star
Asterias forbesi

Giant Green Anemone
Anthopleura xanthogrammica

Aggregating Anemone
Anthopleura elegantissima

Striped Shore Crab
Pachygrapsus crassipes

Blue-Banded Hermit Crab
Pagurus samuelis

ACTIVITY: NATURE ART

At the beach, you can get creative with natural materials. Among the sand, shells, seaweed, driftwood, and other items that you can find on the beach, there are many different colors, shapes, and textures to play with. Try collecting some interesting items and making a beautiful arrangement. Of course, you can also build a sandcastle, a classic beach activity! Before you go home, please flatten any structures and fill in any holes in the sand, as these can be tripping hazards for other visitors.

You can check out examples of larger art installations made of ocean plastic on the websites for **Washed Ashore** (www.washedashore.org) and **Plastic Ocean Project** (www.plasticoceanproject.org /outreach-through-art.html).

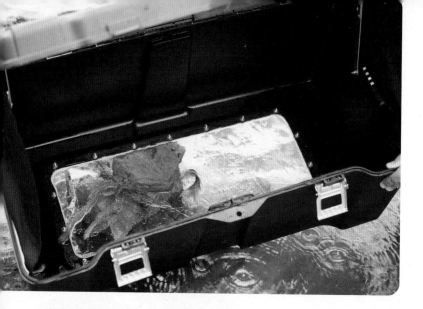

ACTIVITY: MAKE A BATHYSCOPE

What is a Bathyscope

A bathyscope is a simple tool that allows you to see underwater without the sun's glare obscuring the surface. You can make one at home and bring it to the beach with you to help explore the shallows beneath the waves.

What you need

- Empty can or container (can be metal or plastic)
- Plastic wrap (to make this activity more sustainable, use rinsed plastic wrap or clear plastic that has already been used on leftovers or in a box you received through the mail)
- Rubber band
- Tape
- Scissors
- Can opener (if you opt to use a metal can)

Instructions

Using your scissors (for a plastic container) or a can opener (with a parent's help on a metal can), remove the bottom so that both sides of the container are open. Next, use masking tape around the edges to make it safe from sharp edges, so you don't have to worry about cutting yourself later. Layer the plastic over one open end of the container, holding it in place with the masking tape.

To use your bathyscope at the beach, submerge the end of the can or container with the plastic in place beneath the water, but look through the other end above the surface. You should be able to see much better! Keep a count of what you observe so you can record in your nature journal (page 130).

ACTIVITY: QUADRAT SAMPLING

Do you want to train to be a scientist someday? You can! All you need is curiosity and a hula hoop.

Instructions

Bring your hula hoop to the beach. Choose your general "study area"—the part of the beach you are most interested in. (For this activity, it is helpful to be on the beach, not in the water.) Randomly toss the hula hoop and let it settle (scientists use squares for this purpose, which is why it is called a quadrat, but hula hoops work just as well!).

Count all the different plants and animals you see within the hula hoop, and keep a list on a piece of paper or in your nature journal.

Throw the hula hoop four more times (or as many times as you like!), counting all the plants and animals each time.

How many different species did you see? How many of *each* species did you see? Practice making bar graphs in your notebook or your computer to see which species was the most or least abundant in your study area.

ACTIVITY: KEEP A NATURE JOURNAL

What You Need

- A journal
- A pen, colored pencils, and/or other writing implements
- Field guides
- Binoculars
- A camera

Keeping a nature journal is one of the best ways to develop your observation skills and keep your notes safe year after year.

There are many ways to keep a nature journal, and you can choose which method works best for you. If you're not an artist, that's okay! The process of observing and recording what you see is the most important part.

Instructions

1. Keep lists and take notes.
Each time you head to a beach or coastal spot, what do you see? Note the time of day, the weather, and which critters and plants you observe. Take some notes. Are birds flying or feeding? Are crabs in their holes or on the sand? Do you see anything in the surf line? Make sure you include

the date, so you can look back and notice patterns about what you see in the different seasons.

2. **Make sketches.** Sketching is one of the best ways to learn field marks for different species. What do shells look like on the sand or in your hand? What do birds look like when they are flying or standing on the beach? What crab colors can you see close up versus when you are far away? Sketch your favorite species over and over to get a feel for how they change from season to season, or seek new species every time!

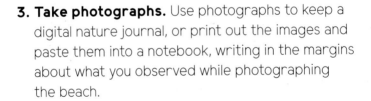

3. **Take photographs.** Use photographs to keep a digital nature journal, or print out the images and paste them into a notebook, writing in the margins about what you observed while photographing the beach.

ACTIVITY: COMMUNITY SCIENCE

Community science (also known as *citizen science*) is when members of the public participate in scientific work. Science enthusiasts can volunteer their time to collect important data, for example, by reporting observations of birds, submitting photos of the coastline, and counting horseshoe crabs. Often a community science project is overseen by professional scientists. Community science projects can record vast amounts of data that otherwise may not have been possible to collect. Every day, people engaging in community science helps scientists do research to better understand the environment around us and what is happening to plant and animal populations.

eBird

Birders across the United States and around the world record their observations and submit them to this, a community science project run by the Cornell Lab of Ornithology. Available on the website (ebird.org) or the mobile app, eBird allows individuals to record information about the birds they see: what species, where the bird was found, and how many

individuals were spotted. As of 2021, community scientists have submitted more than 100 million observations! The data is used by researchers and scientists to learn more about how birds migrate, how climate change affects their populations, and where they live at different times of year. Birders use the app to decide where they should go birding, or where they should look for specific species.

Reporting your sightings on beaches is especially important, because beaches act as essential stopping points for so many migratory species, and cataloging them can help scientists track this spring and fall movement. In addition, many rare birds breed on our beaches in the summer, including Least Terns, Black Skimmers, Piping Plovers, oystercatchers, and more. If you see one, you can help researchers measure their breeding success every season. Be careful, though!

These birds are protected by state and federal laws, so you need to make sure you stay out of their marked nesting colonies and don't get too close.

Note: If you record birds in your yard or another place that is private, you can "hide" your observations so people do not see the location. Otherwise, your data is public.

iNaturalist

This website and mobile app (inaturalist.org) also collects observations from around the world about all kinds of species. As they explain on their website, "Every observation can contribute to biodiversity

science, from the rarest butterfly to the most common backyard weed. We share your findings with scientific data repositories like the Global Biodiversity Information Facility to help scientists find and use your data. All you have to do is observe."

Not sure what species you are seeing? No problem! iNaturalist has a cool feature that lets other naturalists help you with identifying plants and animals. It also has a special computer program that can help identify your photos automatically. It's not perfect, but it's often a good start!

Horseshoe Crab Counts

In Delaware, New Jersey, and Florida, community scientists can look for horseshoe crabs to help scientists learn more about this unique species. Dedicated volunteers learn how to monitor the horseshoe crabs along the beach. The efforts of community scientists help scientists understand population trends and behaviors of these animals.

Horseshoe crabs are an important part of the food web, and they support many fish species, shorebirds, and loggerhead turtles. Medical researchers discovered that a substance in horseshoe crab blood can help test medicines and vaccines.

Scientists are looking for a way to make that substance in a laboratory so that it doesn't need to be harvested from horseshoe crabs anymore.

For more information about horseshoe crab counts, see the **Florida Fish and Wildlife Commission** (myfwc.com/news/all-news/horseshoe-220) and, in Delaware and New Jersey, **The Horseshoe Crab** (www.horseshoecrab.org/act/count.html).

Plastic Pollution

Community scientists can use their smartphone to take a photo of plastic litter and upload it to the **Open Litter Map** (www.openlittermap.com). This global database collects and shares information on the amount and type of litter to help the world make the changes needed to stop plastic pollution.

Coastline Change

Community scientists can also use their smartphones to monitor how coastlines change over time. **Coast-Snap** (www.coastsnap.com) has set up more than 200 stations in 21 countries, where a special camera cradle helps individuals take photos, all in precisely the same direction. This makes it possible for scientists to collect all the photos, then assemble a time lapse of the coastline and study how it changes over time as a result of weather events, sea level rise, and human activities.

Beach-Friendly Organizations

Many people in a variety of organizations work to study and care for habitats and wildlife in the beaches and oceans. These organizations offer activities for the public to learn and get involved in science and stewardship. To continue learning, check out the following organizations and more:

- **National Audubon Society:** www.audubon.org
- **National Oceanic and Atmospheric Administration:** www.noaa.gov
- **National Estuarine Research Reserve System:** coast.noaa.gov/nerrs
- **Ocean Conservancy:** www.oceanconservancy.org
- **Surfrider Foundation:** www.surfrider.org

Willet

State Seashells

ALABAMA
Johnstone's junonia
Scaphella junonia

CONNECTICUT, MISSISSIPPI, AND VIRGINIA
Eastern Oyster
Crassostrea virginica

DELAWARE
Channeled Whelk
Busycotypus canaliculatus

FLORIDA
Horse Conch
Triplofusus papillosus

GEORGIA AND NEW JERSEY
Knobbed Whelk
Busycon carica

MASSACHUSETTS
New England Neptune
Neptunea lyrata ssp. *decemcostata*

State Seashells *(continued)*

NEW YORK
Bay Scallop
Argopecten irradians

NORTH CAROLINA
Scotch Bonnet
Semicassis granulata

OREGON
Oregon Hairy Triton
Fusitriton oregonensis

RHODE ISLAND
Quahog
Mercenaria mercenaria

SOUTH CAROLINA
Lettered Olive
Oliva sayana

TEXAS
Lightning Whelk
Sinistrofulgur perversum

State Marine Mammals

CALIFORNIA
Gray Whale
Eschrichtius robustus

FLORIDA
Manatee
Trichechus manatus latirostris

GEORGIA AND MASSACHUSETTS
North Atlantic Right Whale
Eubalaena glacialis

RHODE ISLAND
Harbor Seal
Phoca vitulina

SOUTH CAROLINA
Bottlenose Dolphin
Tursiops truncatus

WASHINGTON
Orca
Orcinus orca

Recommended Reading

INSPIRING READS ABOUT CONSERVATION AND SCIENCE

Bill Nye's Great Big World of Science, by Bill Nye and Gregory Mone

The Book of Hope: A Survival Guide for Trying Times, by Jane Goodall and Douglas Abrams

Braiding Sweetgrass: Indigenous Wisdom, Scientific Knowledge, and the Teachings of Plants, by Robin Wall Kimmerer

Going Blue: A Teen Guide to Saving Our Oceans, Lakes, Rivers & Wetlands, by Cathryn Berger Kaye, MA, and Philippe Cousteau

Last Chance to See, by Douglas Adams and Mark Carwardine

A Sand County Almanac, by Aldo Leopold

Silent Spring, by Rachel Carson

BOOKS ABOUT SCIENTISTS

Life in the Ocean: The Story of Oceanographer Sylvia Earle, by Claire A. Nivola

Manfish: A Story of Jacques Cousteau, by Jennifer Berne

Rachel Carson: Pioneer of Ecology, by Kathleen V. Kudlinski

Secrets of the Sea: The Story of Jeanne Power, Revolutionary Marine Scientist, by Evan Griffith

Shark Lady: The True Story of How Eugenie Clark Became the Ocean's Most Fearless Scientist, by Jess Keating

FIELD GUIDES

Backyard Birding for Kids, by Erika Zambello

Fossils for Kids, by Dan R. Lynch

Insects & Bugs for Kids, by Jaret C. Daniels

The Sibley Guide to Birds, by David Allen Sibley

Photo Credits *(continued from page 2)*

All photos copyright by their prospective photographers:
Susannah Anderson: 89 (bottom right); **ChrisMcV/iNaturalist:** 111 (left); **Casey Cunningham:** 120 (bottom left); **Hannah Floyd:** 82 (top right); **Joanna Gilkeson/USFWS:** 109 (top left); **Alex Heyman:** 120 (bottom right); **Jana Jackson:** 82 (top left); **Al Kordesch:** 81 (bottom left), 120 (top right); **NASA, Norman Kuring, MODIS Ocean Team:** 23; **NOAA:** 22, 53 (bottom left), 139 (MA); **NOAA, Greg McFall:** 77 (top); **Oregon Coast Aquarium:** 93 (middle left); **Peter Pearsall/U.S. Fish and Wildlife Service:** 81 (top right), 113 (top); **UNSW Water Research Laboratory:** 137; and **Erika Zambello:** 130, 131.

Page 21, Figure modified by D. Reed from image by J. Wallace and S. Vogel, *El Niño and Climate Prediction*. Image courtesy of Sanctuary Quest 2002, NOAA/OER.

Page 83, top - "Ostrea Lurida" (unaltered) by Flickr user VIUDeepBay licensed according to an Attribution 2.0 Creative Commons License (https://creativecommons.org/licenses/by/2.0/); original image via: https://www.flickr.com/photos/44080391@N07/5778358466

Page 84, top right - "Urchin Shell" (unaltered) by Flickr user Ed Beirman licensed according to an Attribution 2.0 Creative Commons License (https://creativecommons.org/licenses/by/2.0/); original image via: https://www.flickr.com/photos/edbierman/2922944115/

Page 90, top - "Kelp Crab (Pugettia productus)" (unaltered) by Flickr user Jerry Kirkhart licensed according to an Attribution 2.0 Creative Commons License (https://creativecommons.org/licenses/by/2.0/); original image via: https://www.flickr.com/photos/jkirkhart35/423767585

Page 93, bottom right - "Starry Flounder" (unaltered) by iNaturalist user leecain licensed according to an Attribution 2.0 Creative Commons License (https://creativecommons.org/licenses/by/2.0/); original image via: https://www.inaturalist.org/observations/4872854

Page 112, top left - "Surfgrass & feather boa kelp, North Moonstone SLO.jpg" (altered) by Peter D. Tillman licensed according to an Attribution 3.0 Unported Creative Commons License (https://creativecommons.org/licenses/by/3.0/deed.en); original image via: https://commons.wikimedia.org/wiki/File:Surfgrass_%26_feather_boa_kelp,_North_Moonstone_SLO.jpg

Page 120, top left - "Eastern Beaded Chiton Chaetopleura apiculata" (unaltered) by Austin Smith licensed according to an Attribution 4.0 International Creative Commons License (https://creativecommons.org/licenses/by/4.0/); original image via: https://www.inaturalist.org/observations/108537570

Page 121, bottom right - "Asterias forbesi_(11862)_0550" (unaltered) by Robert Aguilar, Smithsonian Environmental Research Center licensed according to an Attribution 2.0 Generic Creative Commons License (https://creativecommons.org/licenses/by/2.0/); original image via: I1

Page 126 - "4G7A9342" by Foxcroft Academy licensed according to an Attribution 2.0 Generic Creative Commons License (https://creativecommons.org/licenses/by/2.0/); original image via: https://www.flickr.com/photos/foxcroftacademy/36186033336/

Images used under license from Shutterstock.com:
2009fotofriends: 41 (13); **2Dvisualize:** 48 (middle left); **A Cotton Photo:** 70 (right); **A Wandering Soul:** 89 (top right); **A. Viduetsky:** 99 (top left), 104 (middle left); **aabeele:** 61 (top left); **ABEMOS:** 34 (23); **Adam Gladstone:** 48 (bottom left); **Agami Photo Agency:** 57

(middle left), 59 (top right), 60 (both middle), 61 (bottom right), 64 (middle right), 99 (bottom left), 102 (bottom left); **Alan Dunn:** 104 (bottom left); **Alessandro De Maddalena:** 69 (top left); **Alex Cooper Photography:** 103 (bottom right); **Alexey Masliy:** 140 (SC); **Alisha Newton:** 14 (oyster reefs); **alitellioglu:** 99 (middle right); **Allen McDavid Stoddard:** 73 (top right); **Andrea Izzotti:** 96 (top right); **Andrey Armyagov:** 57 (bottom left); **Andy Konieczny:** 41 (3); **Anthony Julien:** 85; **aragami12345s:** 29; **Arina P Habich:** 75 (top left); **Artazum:** 41 (24); **Ashley Meers:** 55 (top right); **Aydin-Akin:** 51 (top left), 140 (TX); **Bandersnatch:** 90 (bottom left); **Barbara Ash:** 92 (top right), 95 (left); **Beata Tabak:** 119 (top left); **Benjamin Albiach Galan:** 57 (top left); **Bill Kennedy:** 122 (top left); **Bill Pruitt:** 105 (bottom); **Blacqbook:** 133; **blandas71:** 34 (6); **BlueBarronPhoto:** 101 (top right); **Bonnie Taylor Barry:** 34 (2), 47 (bottom left), 52 (middle left); **Bouke Atema:** 59 (middle left); **Brian Lasenby:** 64 (bottom right), 100 (middle left), 102 (top left), 104 (bottom right); **Brittany Mason:** 75 (top right); **BW Folsom:** 140 (RI); **Carl Olsen:** 103 (top left); **Catherine Eckert:** 75 (bottom right); **Charles Siu:** 88 (bottom right); **Chase Dekker:** 14 (Blue Whale); **Cheryl Casey:** 34 (7); **Chintla:** 41 (8); **Chris Anson:** 25 (middle); **Chris Klonowski:** 63 (middle right), 64 (top right); **Christophe Merceron:** 60 (bottom right); **Christopher PB:** 74 (top right); **ChWeiss:** 78 (bottom left); **Cire notrevo:** 34 (1); **Claudia G Cooper:** 41 (21); **Colin D. Young:** 35 (26); **Colin Seddon:** 66 (top right); **Colnago 95310:** 43 (3rd); **CornelPutan:** 114 (bottom right); **CSNafzger:** 41 (17); **Damsea:** 54 (bottom left), 55 (top left); **Dancestrokes:** 43 (2nd); **Daniel Lamborn:** 71 (top right); **Daniel NovakL:** 52 (middle left); **Daniel Wright98:** 47 (bottom right); **Danita Delimont:** 41 (23), 111 (right), 112 (bottom left), 122 (top right); **Darryl Vest:** 138; **David A Litman:** 88 (top right), 92 (top left), 96 (top left); **David Carbo:** 110 (bottom); **David Osborn:** 30, 60 (bottom left), 64 (middle left), 100 (top right); **Delpixel:** 106 (left); **Dennis Jacobsen:** 62 (top right); **Dennis W Donohue:** 105 (top); **divedog:** 13 (seagrass meadow); **digidreamgrafix:** 34 (4); **Diver_adventures:** 54 (bottom right); **Dolores M. Harvey:** 109 (bottom right); **Donna Carpenter:** 35 (32); **Dray van Beeck:** 72 (top left); **Drew McArthur:** 78 (bottom left); **Drone Stock Pros:** 34 (18); **Edmund Lowe Photography:** 12 (estuaries); **elakazal:** 89 (top left); **Elliotte Rusty Harold:** 63 (bottom right), 73 (bottom right); **EQRoy:** 48 (bottom right); **Eric M. Schmitz:** 41 (16); **Erni:** 61 (top right), 101 (bottom right); **Estevan Silvestri:** 54 (top right); **Ethan Daniels:** 55 (bottom), 76 (middle left), 112 (bottom right), 113 (top); **140 (NY); **Eugene Kalenkovich:** 67 (top); **Eva McDermott:** 41 (9); **Fabian Junge:** 121 (bottom left); **FarsyR:** 24 (quartz sand); **Fashion-Stock.com:** 41 (5); **Felix Mizioznikov:** 34 (10); **Finley Del:** 72 (bottom right); **FloridaStock:** 60 (top right); **FotosForTheFuture:** 35 (25); **Francisco Blanco:** 11 (mangroves); **Frank Wickstrom:** 69 (middle right); **frantisekhojdysz:** 71 (middle right); **Gerald Peplow:** 119 (bottom right); **Gerry Bishop:** 76 (bottom left); **Geza Farkas:** 140 (NC); **Gilbert S. Grant:** 139 (CT/VA); **GinaVector:** 139 (AL); **Ginette Leclair:** 76 (top left); **Glenn Price:** 102 (bottom right); **Golbay:** 69 (bottom left); **Good_Stock:** 28; **Greg Amptman:** 65 (top), 121 (top left); **GUDKOV ANDREY:** 66 (bottom left); **haireena:** 48 (top left); **HannaTor:** 41 (6); **Harry Collins Photography:** 34 (24); **haveseen:** 35 (28 & 30); **HelloRF Zcool:** 88 (bottom left); **iam_seanmcvey:** 44; **Ian Scott:** 71 (top left), 72 (top right); **Imogen Warren:** 99 (middle left); **Inbound Horizons:** 41 (19); **Ingrid Maasik:** 49 (bottom); **InLoveWithSeaglass:** 79 (top); **IrinaK:** 68 (Redfish), 69 (middle left), 87 (right); **Iryna Kalamurza:** 108 (bottom left); **Jan-Dirk Hansen:** 141 (CA); **Janet Griffin:** 57 (middle right); **Jarous:** 76 (bottom left); **Jason Patrick Ross:** 34 (5); **JB Manning:** 57 (middle right); **Jerry Kirkhart:** 122 (bottom right); **Jesus_Miguel:** 60 (top left); **JIANG HONGYAN:** 80; **Joao Virissimo:** 139 (DE); **Joe Belanger:** 91 (bottom right), 93 (top left); **joern_k:** 72 (bottom left); **Joke van Eeghem:** 34 (9); **Jon Bilous:** 35 (31); **Joni Hanebutt:** 50 (bottom left); **Judith Lienert:** 63 (bottom left); **Jukka Jantunen:** 62 (top left); **Justin DeRosa:** 38 (top); **KarenHBlack:** 73 (bottom left); **Karl R. Martin:** 104 (middle right); **kaschibo:** 71 (bottom right); **KatarzynaZakowska:** 114 (bottom left); **KatieHerron:** 50 (top right); **Keith Pritchard:** 98 (bottom right); **kelly reilly:** 65 (bottom); **Kelly vanDellen:** 43 (bottom); **Kenneth Keifer:** 10 (Yellow-crowned Night Heron); **Kevin Ruck:** 34 (21); **Kevin White Photographer:** 16 (top); **KGrif:** 13 (middle); **Khairil Azhar Junos:** 69 (top right); **Kharlanov Evgeny:** 124 (bottom); **klerik78:** 35 (map), 41 (map), 117 (maps); **KrimKate:** 53 (top left); **Krumpelman Photography:** 101 (middle left);

Kurkul: 82 (bottom right); **Kyle J Little:** 34 (22); **Larina Marina:** 136; **Laurence Appaix:** 107 (top right); **lazyllama:** 78 (top left); **Leith Holtzman:** 15 (Whale Shark); **Lena Ivanova:** 139 (FL); **LeStudio:** 35 (29); **Lidiya Oleandra:** 3; **Liz DLT:** 88 (top left); **Lonny Garris:** 59 (middle right); **Lost_in_the_Midwest:** 11 (top), 76 (middle right); **lunamarina:** 24 (coquina, orange), 34 (11); **Lynne Neuman:** 34 (16); **Lysogor Roman:** 135; **MagicBones:** 93 (top right); **Margaret.Wiktor:** 34 (20); **Mariusz S. Jurgielewicz:** 41 (11); **Mark A. McCaffrey:** 93 (bottom left); **Martin Prochazkacz:** 74 (top left); **Martina Birnbaum:** 41 (15); **Mateusz Sciborski:** 59 (bottom left); **Matt Binding:** 62 (bottom left); **Matt9122:** 70 (left); **Maverick-Diving:** 119 (top right); **Mel Kowasic:** 107 (middle left); **Menno Schaefer:** 64 (bottom left); **Meredith Lamb:** 52 (top left); **Merrimon Crawford:** 100 (top left); **Mia2you:** 34 (13); **Michael Benard:** 122 (bottom left); **Michael R Brown:** 37 (bottom); **Michael Sean OLeary:** 39 (top); **Mila Drumeva:** 63 (middle left); **mljphotography:** 121 (middle right); **Moarly:** 107 (top left); **Mogens Trolle:** 96 (bottom); **Molishka:** 68 (Needlefish); **MR. BUDDEE WIANGNGORN:** 24 (top); **My Life Graphic:** 134; **Myotis:** 114 (top); **Nancy Hixson:** 106 (right); **Natalia Kuzmina:** 51 (bottom left); **Natalia Paklina:** 62 (bottom right); **Nature's Charm:** 41 (4), 86 (top); **NatureDiver:** 140 (OR); **Nelyan:** 74 (middle left); **Nick Kashenko:** 94 (top); **Nick Pecker:** 98 (top left), 98 (bottom left), 107 (bottom left); **Noah Strycker:** 61 (middle left); **Odeta Lukoseviciute:** 124 (top right); **Oleg Kovtun Hydrobio:** 74 (bottom right); **pamala davis:** 125 (top); **Paolo Tralli:** 24 (black sand); **Paul Reeves Photography:** 100 (bottom right); **Paula Cobleigh:** 33; **Paula Montenegro Stock:** 35 (27); **PETER LAKOMY:** 34 (19); **Peter Leahy:** 14 (Florida coral reef), 54 (top left), 109 (bottom left), 110 (top); **Peter Schwarz:** 101 (top left); **Peter6172:** 102 (middle right); **Philip Garner:** 92 (bottom right); **Phitha Tanpairoj:** 41 (7); **picchu productions:** 41 (10); **Picmin:** 84 (top left); **Pierre Leclerc:** 41 (22); **pisaphotography:** 26, 34 (15); **PKKoala:** 89 (bottom left); **Podolnaya Elena:** 92 (bottom left); **Porco_Rosso:** 13 (kelp forest), 66 (bottom right), 141 (GA/MA); **Rabbitti:** 66 (top left), 141 (RI); **Rachel Blaser:** 112 (middle right); **Radoslaw Lecyk:** 41 (14); **Rafal Michal Gadomski:** 36; **Randy Bjorklund:** 83 (bottom); **Realest Nature:** 34 (3); **Rich Carey:** 17 (green sea turtle); **Rigucci:** 41 (18); **Ronnie Chua:** 41 (2); **Roo Pix:** 75 (bottom left); **Rotorhead 30A Productions:** 25 (bottom); **Ruben Martinez Barricarte:** 71 (bottom left); **Rudmer Zwerver:** 62 (middle left); **Russell Marshall:** 102 (middle left); **Rusya007:** 94 (bottom); **Ruth Peterkin:** 34 (8); **Sakis Lazarides:** 57 (top right), 119 (bottom left); **Samib123:** 129; **SanderMeertinsPhotography:** 100 (middle right); **serg_dibrova:** 74 (bottom left); **SherryLee:** 103 (bottom left); **Simon Dannhauer:** 27; **Simonas Minkevicius:** 64 (top left), 102 (top right); **Simone Hogan:** 10 (tidepools); **slowmotiongli:** 69 (bottom right), 93 (middle right); **SNC Art and More:** 12 (salt marshes), 121 (middle left); **Sonja Filitz:** 37 (top); **Sputnik Aloysius:** 90 (bottom right); **Stephen B. Goodwin:** 47 (top right); **Steve Bower:** 73 (top left), 77 (bottom); **Steve Byland:** 61 (bottom left), 81 (bottom right), 99 (top right), 101 (bottom left), 103 (top right); **steve estvanik:** 112 (middle left); **stevehullphotography:** 87 (left); **Stockimo:** 84 (bottom left); **Stubblefield Photography:** 62 (middle left); **Sundry Photography:** 121 (top right); **SunflowerMomma:** 34 (12), 52 (bottom right), 68 (Pompano), 84 (bottom right), 91 (top); **Susan Hodgson:** 100 (bottom left); **Susanne Pommer:** 34 (14); **Take Photo:** 17 (top); **Tamara Kulikova:** 49 (top), 79 (bottom); **Tania Khalaziy:** 125 (bottom); **Tarpan:** 107 (middle right); **The World Traveller:** 81 (top left); **ThelmaElaine:** 82 (bottom left); **Tim Balcomb:** 91 (bottom left); **tim elliott:** 98 (top right); **Timmothy Mcdade:** 95 (right); **Tomas Kotouc:** 141 (FL); **Tory Kallman:** 67 (bottom), 108 (top left & top right), 141 (SC & WA); **Tupungato:** 10 (mudflats); **vagabond54:** 104 (top left); **valda butterworth:** 50 (top left); **Victor1153:** 48 (middle right); **Victoria Ditkovsky:** 41 (12); **Vivian Fung:** 41 (1); **Vladimir Wrangel:** 68 (Tarpon); **Wandering Nature:** 74 (middle right); **Wildnerdpix:** 123; **William Silver:** 34 (17); **wing-wing:** 6; **Wolfgang Kruck:** 59 (top left); **Wollertz:** 86 (bottom); **Xiao Zhou:** 43 (top), 47 (top left), 48 (top right), 51 (top right & bottom right), 52 (top right & bottom left), 53 (top right), 139 (GA/NJ); **Yes058 Montree Nanta:** 25 (top); **Yingna Cai:** 46; **Zack Frank:** 116; **Zhukova Valentyna:** 41 (20); and **Zi Magine:** 71 (middle left).

Learning About Science and Nature Is Fun!

Get hooked on the most appealing aspects of nature. The Simple Introductions to Science series takes a scientific look at the natural world. Each book serves as a basic introduction and a field identification guide. When applicable, the books also present how-to instructions for finding and collecting. The series' colorful, appealing design includes plenty of full-color photographs and illustrations, while headers and short blocks of text make for easy reading.

Complete your collection with the other books in this educational, entertaining series.

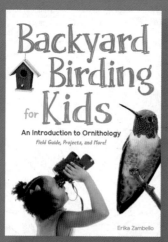

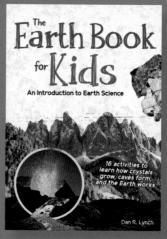

Backyard Birding for Kids
136 pg · $12.95 · 9781647552237

The Earth Book for Kids
176 pg · $12.95 · 781647552831

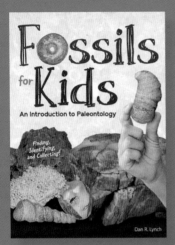

Fossils for Kids
188 pg · $12.95 · 9781591939399

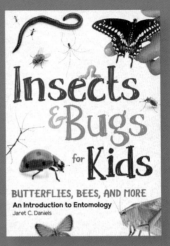

Insects & Bugs for Kids
128 pg · $12.95 · 9781647551643

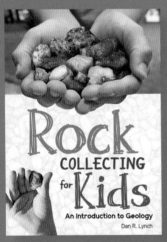

Rock Collecting for Kids
144 pg · $12.95 · 9781591937739

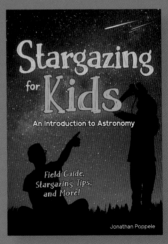

Stargazing for Kids
176 pg · $12.95 · 9781647551346

About the Authors

STEPHANIE PANLASIGUI

In her home state of California, Stephanie grew up 7 miles from the Pacific Ocean, where she enjoyed spending time with her family while swimming, spotting dolphins, and hiking on the bluffs. Stephanie began her career as a naturalist, guiding children to explore redwood forests, buckeye groves, tidepools, and sandy beaches. Now she works on understanding how restoring and protecting habitats can support thriving human and wildlife populations. She holds a master's degree in environmental management from Duke University and a bachelor's degree in environmental sciences from the University of California, Berkeley.

ERIKA ZAMBELLO

From her home base in North Florida, Erika has explored hundreds of parks, reserves, and wildlife refuges across the Southeast and around the country. She was a National Geographic Young Explorer and serves on the board of the *National Parks Traveler* website. She holds a master's degree in environmental management from Duke University and a master's degree in strategic communication from the University of West Florida. As a writer, she has been featured in *National Geographic Adventure*, *National Geographic Voices*, *Backpacker*, *Florida Sportsman*, and other publications.